Don't Leave Money on The Table

Negotiation Strategies for Women in Male-Dominated Industries

Jacqueline Twillie, MBA

Dedication

This book did dedicated to the amazing women in my life. My mother, grandmother, aunts, sisters, nieces and goddaughters. May you always know your value.

Acknowledgements

With the support of my family and close friends I found the inspiration to write this book. Special thank you to Derrick for being supportive, I could not have finished this project without you.

Contents

Intro - If you don't ask, you won't get

Many women have subscribed to the belief that if you work really hard and keep your head down, someone will notice and give you a promotion or a raise. I hate to be the bearer of bad news but if you don't ask you will not get. The best advocate for your career and leadership journey is you. While it's important to have strong relationships within your network and company, you must have sponsors and mentors who can guide you and open doors for you. The ultimate responsibility for negotiating whether it's a business deal or salary is up to you.

According to Sara Laschever and Linda Babcock, co-authors of the book Women Don't Ask: Negotiations and the Gender Divide, by not negotiating a first salary, an individual stands to lose more than $500,000 by age 60 — and men are more than four times as likely as women to negotiate a first salary. It's wise to research the market rate before accepting a job offer, and it's also important to understand that most companies expect you to negotiate. Because of that, it is rare that the first job offer is the best job offer. Given that it will benefit the entry-level professional to thoroughly research the full compensation benefits of the company that she is preparing to negotiate with. Talk to members of the professional association of your industry as well as college alumni networks to get the inside scoop about a company's negotiation strategy and the types of packages offered.

Contrary to what some may believe women are excellent negotiators. When it comes to representational negotiations, women outperform men. However, when it's time for a woman to advocate for herself, she does not have the same confidence. We're going to get into some of those reasons in this book, but more importantly, the solutions for how you can become a better advocate for yourself and take agency to ask for what you want.

Your career trajectory depends on you advocating for yourself. As an individual contributor, being able to position yourself to grow to the highest level in your profession doesn't happen by accident. As a manager, you're able to advocate for the resources, tools, and support that you need to be effective in your leadership journey. In your team, it's to achieve company objectives. This book will give you principles to use for negotiations as you negotiate in your professional life.

Why I focus on negotiation as a partial solution to the Gender Wage Gap

The gender wage gap is often referred to as the gap in earnings between men and women. One of the common metrics is the median income of men and women divided. While there are numerous causes to the wage gap, it's magnified for women of color. Part of the wage gap is unexplained as well as direct pay discrimination Adding to that, it's pervasive in numerous professions from housekeeping to physicians. Within the highest-earning industries, women are the minority in the workplace. These factors are vast and will not be solved with a single solution. To eliminate the wage gap, it will take persistent dedication to address all the factors that contribute to the gap. I decided to dedicate my life's work to eliminate the gender wage gap and I do that in two ways. The first is, I teach women how to negotiate effectively so that they don't leave money on the table. The second, I work with corporations in establishing best-practices to retain and enhance the skills of women leaders within male-dominated industries. We know that the people at the heads of organizations get paid the most and women are not ascending to the top of the leadership ranks fast enough. According to Fortune Magazine, women who lead Fortune 500 companies reached its peak in 2017 with less than 8% of women CEOs. Women have to overcome the decades-long rules that leadership is reserved for white males. There are numerous well-researched studies that confer that diversity in leadership reduces a company's risk and increases profitability. The business case to have a diverse Executive leadership is there, and a byproduct of placing more women in top leadership roles is the reduction of the wage gap.

The American Association of University Women has conducted decades of research surrounding the factors of the wage gap. One of the many causes that lead to the wage gap is one factor that can be immediately addressed. Many women simply don't ask for more when offered a job. There is a valid reason to have concerns of backlash when negotiating your salary. However, many employers do expect some form of negotiation. With this assumption, the first job offer presented typically is not the best offer the employer can offer. When women are equipped with the knowledge that the first offer is rarely the best offer, it removes one barrier to negotiate and ask for more. Negotiation is a skill that can be developed just like anything else with repetition. The more you practice and focus on it, the stronger the skill will become. This book explains the complexity of negotiation and the societal norms that create additional hurdles for women who wish to use this skill to increase earnings and claim agency. While the problems are prevalent, women do successfully overcome these challenges with dedicated focus. With this book, my hope is that you will read it and share it with the women and girls in your life so that collectively we reduce the opportunities to leave money on the table.

Know Your Value

> "I am not lucky. You know what I am? I am smart, I am talented, I take advantage of the opportunities that come my way and I work really, really hard. Don't call me lucky. Call me a badass." — *Shonda Rhimes*

There are so many clichés that have been turned into memes and headlines about knowing your value. The chapter in this book that has the most weight is this chapter, and it will help you to identify the tangible ways in which you bring value to the party that you're negotiating with. Without a firm understanding of the value that you add to the party that you were negotiating with, you will settle for less than what you're worth and risk not being taken as seriously by the other party.

When a woman receives an invitation to pitch a business or interview for a job, she is in that position because she has skills, products, or services that are of a value. There may be factors that will lead her to question herself such as:

- am I good enough

- will I do a good job

- do I have all of the skills it takes to deliver the results that will be expected

Those questions must be addressed in order to negotiate the best deal. The simple answer to the questions, "Am I good enough?" or "Can I do it?", that swirl about is "Yes, you can." Looking to your knowledge and experience shown on the resume, LinkedIn profile, and past experiences, seek as evidence to prove "Yes, you can. The things that you have done before have given you the knowledge to figure out task and complete the task you were hired for.

When a company hires a person to fill an open position, they are looking to gain the value of knowledge and expertise from that person to be able to perform at a high-level that will consistently move the company towards achieving and exceeding its stated goals. A question that isn't asked enough by the interviewee in the interview process is "How do you envision the person that you will hire will add value to the team and the projects that are most important to this division?"

Many job applicants and business deal-makers fail to get an understanding of the other party's needs before expressing the value that they can add. As a result of the lack of information related to the other party's needs, many women fall into the trap of expressing everything they can do instead of highlighting the most relevant aspects of their skill set in relation to the business needs. Preparing a list of open-ended questions prior to engaging in a negotiation and using a combination of your network and online research to answer those questions is a starting point to anticipate the needs of the other party. The practice of establishing a set of open-ended questions in advance will prompt you when in a face-to-face meeting to ask similar open-ended questions so that you can gain insight and information that will allow you to express how you add value to the other party.

In expressing your value, unless the deal is seeking someone who is Jill-of-all-trades, you need a certain level of detail to adequately express who you are, what you do, and how you can deliver results for the other party. In response to a clapback culture, many people can subscribe to philosophy I'm checking other people for not recognizing their value but failing to also understand that communication surrounding a valuable exchange has to go beyond surface-level issues and address the concerns and problems of each party before terms of a deal are laid out on a table.

Knowing your value is not:

- A singular credential such as a certification or degree

- Time at a job with no track record of learning and contribution

- Doing enough just to get by but consistently being present

- Talking a good game but not backing it up

- Being surrounded by people who deliver significant value

- Networking with the who's who crowd

This is a list of characteristics that will highlight or signify that you own the value that you bring

- Showing up prepared to get a job done

- Seeking to understand before making suggestions or recommendations

- Speaking of your accomplishments in a clear and concise manner

- Backing up suggestions with a strategy

- Ability to connect resources

- Having a reputation as someone who gets things done

- Discipline to be focused on completing tasks

- Taking initiative and being resourceful in the face of challenges

- Ability to bounce back after defeat

- Demanding Excellence for yourself and those around you by being tough and fair

- Eliminating excuses

What do you value? What's really important? A value is what's really important?

Questions to help you articulate your value:

- What type of person do you want to be

- What type of company do you want to work for

- What type of clients do you want to work with

- What type of results do you want to be associated with

> "What do you really value? Until you discover what you really value you won't get what you really want." ~ *Andy Stanley*

According to the Google dictionary value is defined as

Val·u·a·ble /ˈvaly(oō)əb(ə)l/

adjective

adjective: **valuable**

worth a great deal of money.

"a valuable antique"

extremely useful or important.

"my time is valuable"

synonyms:

precious, costly, high-priced, high-cost, expensive, dear, worth its weight in gold, worth a king's ransom, priceless, beyond price, without price, of incalculable value/worth, of inestimable value/worth, of immeasurable value/worth, invaluable, irreplaceable, inestimable; More

noun: valuable; plural noun: valuables

a thing that is of great worth, especially a small item of personal property.

"put all your valuables in the hotel safe"

synonyms:

1. precious items, costly articles, prized possessions, personal effects, treasures

2. "valuables may be left in the hotel safe"

When it comes to women claiming value that they want in negotiations, they tend to downplay their own needs or wants to meet the needs or make the other party feel comfortable. Claiming agency and value is not rude or impolite, it's a characteristic of a confident leader. As you build negotiation skills, get comfortable vocalizing your wants and needs.

As you negotiate begin by establishing the things that you value with a clear understanding of what the other party values are. By carefully considering both parties needs and wants the discussion of exchange of value will be more meaningful. The amount of weight that can be placed on your wants should be related to the level of value that you can add and vice versa with the party that you're negotiating with. Beyond stating the value that you can add, you have to be able to produce receipts related to that success. The relevant types of receipts necessary can be in various forms here are a few examples:

*   LinkedIn or other credible recommendations

*   Industry Awards and/or recognition

*   Resume that speaks directly to the skills or services that you are promoting

*   Testimonials from current or previous clients

*   Business results that can be examined publicly

*   Relationships with people in your industry that can speak on your behalf

- Unapologetic confidence of your skill set while using relevant facts and figures.

When an employer has hired an employee to do a job, the expectation is for the employee to do more than the bare minimum - or just enough to get by. The bare minimum doesn't add significant value and often is not rewarded with increased levels of responsibility and the money that correlates with such responsibility. If a supervisor or peers notice that an employee is constantly texting, or on the phone, or away from work, it can have a negative impact on how that person is valued. It is to the employee's benefit that the supervisor knows that she understands the goals of the organization and that her work consistently focuses on achieving the goals as outlined. Therefore, whatever the employee's role is in achieving that piece of the puzzle, those tasks should be completed with great pride. With any project or task that you're working on within your organization, you should strive to emulate excellence without excuses. Emulating excellence without excuses doesn't mean that you have to be perfect but, it does mean that you do everything to the best of your ability at all times, even when no one is watching. The result of emulating excellence without excuses is a perceived and real increase in the value that you add to the organization. Do not be hesitant to share your contributions with your supervisor in your one-on-one meeting and explain how excited you are to contribute to that very important area of the business. This is a start of how you begin to assess your value to your employer but also showcase to them how you're adding value through the projects that you're working on.

Think of a time where you were in a situation where you really wanted something, but you saw the price and instantly you said, that's okay I no longer want it. In that moment, when you saw the price that item was no longer valuable to you. Alternatively, you could have purchased something, and soon after the purchase or a week later, you have buyer's remorse because when you bought it in the moment, you were excited but then began to second guess your decision. You may begin to question why do I really need this, is it really worth it? When an employer hires a new employee, there may be initial excitement. That person spoke really well and articulated what they could do for the company, in the interim, however, when the employee got into the position, and after the honeymoon phase ended, they noticed that that employer isn't adding as much value as they thought they would during the interview. You don't want that to be you, the person that the employer is having second thoughts about. You won't always be excited about your work, but you must learn to be disciplined to always produce top quality work. Knowing your value isn't just about an understanding of the business, it is about producing consistently and continuously striving for excellence with the work you deliver.

Many women are uncomfortable speaking about the value they add based on cultural stereotypes - that being braggadocious or confident isn't a "feminine trait." As a result of this common belief, many women work in silence, waiting for someone else to speak on their behalf or advocate for them while sitting in silence, hoping and wishing for more. On the other hand, women are excellent advocates for other people. They encourage others to speak up for themselves and give others the advice to stand up while struggling with the same dilemma themselves. What I have noticed working with women over the years is that they build the confidence to speak up when they have had enough and they're fed up. However, women who get what they want in business speak up early and often. Even if it is uncomfortable or bucks stereotype of what a woman at work should be. To unlock the confidence to speak out before you hit the point where you're fed up is to recognize the value that you add daily.

Here's a pop quiz: are you valuing or devaluing yourself at work?

How do you respond to this statement:

- good job
- nice work
- you're killing it
- keep up the great work
- thanks for doing that

Devaluing statement:

- You don't have to thank me for that
- It was easy
- I can do that in my sleep
- No big deal
- Don't mention it
- That was nothing

Value recognizing statement

- Thank you for recognizing that
- I pride myself on doing a great job
- Thank you
- I appreciate that
- It's nice to hear feedback from the work that I do

- I look forward to contributing more

- It's great to be a recognized member of the team

The way that you respond to compliments at work will signal if you value yourself or not. If you're devaluing the work that you do, it gives other people permission to devalue you as well. Therefore, when it's time for a promotion or raise, if you're consistently downplaying the work that you do, or if you're signaling to your supervisor that you are not ready for more responsibility and you don't contribute effort as everyone else. If you've noticed that you're responding to compliments with devaluing statements, understand that it's going to take time to change your natural response. Don't beat yourself up if after you read this section you notice that you're using devaluing statements. Simply begin to replace with statements that highlight the value you're bringing to your work. The more you practice it, the more natural it will become. It may be helpful to have a trusted advisor or mentor that works with you to help identify moments when you respond with devaluing statements. Request that this feedback be provided in a private setting or via text message or an instant alert. Pay attention to how other women respond to compliments as well if you were the mentor to someone who's using devaluing language. Share with them this section of the book so that they can remove language that does not help them advance at work.

Am I worth that much?

Preparing to give your salary requirement

On many online applications, there is a box that asks for your salary expectations. This is a number that many are not comfortable disclosing, and as a result of the discomfort they do not give enough attention to this section. It is important to note that at the time of this book's publishing, several states have made it illegal to require a job applicant to disclose their salary history. However, it does not prevent the potential employer from asking the question. I believe that the elimination of this salary history requirement is beneficial to women, given that it's proven women across the board are paid less than men. It is still important to strategically answer this question as it is a first anchor in the salary negotiation. Researching the market rate for the position is essential to asking a realistic competitive salary. When it comes to job offers, a lot of women that I have coached through salary negotiations feel as if they have to make a decision instantly. Most employers will not ask a job candidate to make a decision without giving them time to consider the offer. The time span that is allotted for the consideration of a job offer will vary for the employer. However, it's typical to expect between 2-5 days to get back with the employer. The level of seniority of the position that the candidate is applying for can be an indicator as to the length of the time span. For instance, an entry level position may afford a few days consideration, whereas a senior level may be afforded a week or two. To gain the best insight, it is appropriate to ask the person who is extending the offer what their timeline is like and how long you have to respond. When asking how long you can take to think about the offer, re-emphasize your excitement for the position so you don't send mixed signals about your interest in the position.

Consider the following when deciding to accept an offer.

- Market rate / Salary
- Short-term career goals

- Long-term career goals

- Financial goals; not just monthly expenses

- Professional growth opportunity

- Access to organizational resources to achieve position objectives

Don't let fear hold you back from having a conversation about a new salary, promotion, raise, or a business deal.

Avoid Backlash

> "What's the greater risk? Letting go of what people think – or letting go of how I feel, what I believe, and who I am?" ~ *Brene Brown*

Backlash is often considered a double bind for women, considering you're judged by the way you speak up and when you don't it's a missed opportunity. Backlash can be a person retaliating against you for having the savvy and agency to make a request. There is a common saying "you can only control what you can control." That is also true for negotiations while conducting research on the issues on the negotiation. Also gain insight into the people you will negotiate with. Seek to gain an understanding of other people's bias based on your race and gender will help you strategically maneuver throughout the negotiation to avoid and leverage stereotypes while working towards achieving a win-win deal.

There are real concerns that lead to women being

fearful of the consequences of being an advocate for her career advancement. Some of the common types of backlash that women negotiators experience that do not impact their male counterparts are:

- Her relationship with the manager may be damaged

- She will be viewed as needy, difficult to work with, or hard to get along with

- The possibility of being lied to during the negotiation

In the upcoming section, we'll address ways to overcome the challenges of backlash to be able to strongly advocate for self and team members. The consequences of caving in to the fear of backlash can have a significant and lasting impact on the financial future of women according to 2005 report for Science Direct by Hannah Riley Bowles, Linda Babcock, and Lei Lai.

Successful negotiators go into the negotiation prepared to win. Each negotiation is different, and it is important to recognize that a technique that works well in one negotiation might not yield the same results even if you are negotiating with the same person. The factors that lead to getting more of what you want is to know the issues at stake as well as the person(s) you are negotiating with. You'll only be able to negotiate confidently if you are well prepared. Do not get comfortable with previous success negotiating and skip the basic preparation steps or take the "I can wing it" approach. Prior to each negotiation use a checklist which includes understanding the common interest, the value each party adds, the areas of conflict, and creative ways to bridge gaps so that each side walks away saying, "I'll do business with her again."

There's evidence to show that women of color face

more bias, but that doesn't have to deter you. "For example, you do not want the person you are negotiating with to get the perception that you are an "angry black woman" if you show too much emotion during the conversation," she says. "To avoid playing to the stereotype when things are not going the way you planned, take a break instead of losing your cool." One of my favorite strategies to deploy in a heated moment is to request a bathroom break. "By forcing a break during a heated negotiation, you have a chance to collect your thoughts, calm down and come back to the negotiating table focused on presenting the case.

Do's and don'ts when it comes to negotiating pay?

Here are the Do's

- Prepare thoroughly for the negotiation

- Prepare to hear no; and what your counter will be

- Package your request instead of asking issue by issue

- Practice what you want to say

- Practice how you want to say it

- Practice what to say when things don't go as planned

- Ask confidently

- Ask at the right time

- Decide if you want to accept or not

- Evaluate how the negotiation went; what will you do next time?

Don'ts

- Don't lie

- Don't wing it

- Don't skip the preparation

- Don't cut the other person off

- Don't formulate your response as soon as the other person speaks

- Don't rush

- Don't accept without reviewing the written offer

- Don't ignore warning signs

- Don't assume anything

- Don't be afraid to ask questions

POINTS TO REMEMBER DURING NEGOTIATIONS

- Use language that avoids backlash

- Don't give ultimatums

- Do not lie

- Ask for critical support & buy-in

- Find ways to get on the same page

- You can negotiate for work/life integration

- Consider what is possible based on the scope of work

- Listen more than you speak

- Do not be afraid to walk away

In any negotiation, one of the elements that will help you strike a deal is the ability to establish rapport and for each party to understand at some level that they can trust the other party to deliver on what they say they will deliver on. Personal branding is an element that isn't focused on enough when it comes to negotiation as a part of your brand. It isn't just what you say about yourself online. It's what other people say about you when you're not around. With that, your personal brand associated with negotiation carries a lot of weight. An opinion about your negotiation style is developed before you even step in a room based on your previous behavior. Being trustworthy and following through on the things that you say you're going to do is a critical element that will help you to succeed in achieving desired outcomes in negotiation.

To avoid backlash

- Understand how you're being perceived

- What's your negotiation brand, if you have one

- Talk to the other party, not at them

- Listen more than you speak

Think Beyond Salary

When it comes to negotiating with the new job offer or a promotion, think about the tools, resources, and support that you will need to be successful, not just the salary when it comes to negotiating.

When you're going through the interview process, ask questions that will give you insight into the types of challenges that you will be solving in the new role. As your gathering this information in the interview process, take note and think of the things that you will need in order to be successful in the role did you accept the job.

Items that can be included in negotiation beyond salary:

- Job Title

- Additional vacation days

- 401(K) increase match

- New equipment or software

- Tuition reimbursement
- Student loan repayment
- Office space
- Relocation expenses
- Team resources
- Expense allowance
- Performance review period
- Exit Packages
- Leave of absence
- Professional association membership
- Support from senior leadership
- Child Care assistance
- Conference fees

Negotiation Styles

> "Always go into meetings or negotiations with a positive attitude. Tell yourself you're going to make this the best deal for all parties."
> *-Natalie Massenet*

There are five negotiation styles that most people's behaviors fall into. You don't have to know your dominant negotiation style in order to present your request. Remember, negotiation is a like a muscle. The more you use it the stronger it will become, so starting off, if you can't identify your negotiation, do not let that stop you from asking for more. As you become more confident to present request and you negotiate bigger business deals or salaries, you may want to dig deeper into understanding the nuances of negotiation styles so that you not only understand your skill level but you also understand your counterparts negotiation style.

1.   Accommodating (I Lose – You Win)

At first glance, why would anyone want to use this style of negotiating? Who wants to set the other party up to win at her own expense? Whether intentional or not, it's a common negotiation style because so many people use it. However, those who are more focused on the relationship and keeping "the peace," tend to be more accommodating. With this style, one seeks to keep the relationship intact at all costs, even if that means giving away significantly more value than what is being claimed. Some people refer to this style of negotiating as "the peacekeeper" negotiation style.

Women who have traditionally been labeled "nice" at work can also be perceived to be accommodating during negotiations. As a woman negotiating, be aware of how others perceive you because it can shed light into the strategy they may use to negotiate with you. Women tend to be nurturers and are pushed into the "office or work mom" role, often accommodating everyone's needs at the expense of her professional career. Try to avoid this if your desire is to become a C-Suite executive because falling into the accommodating role makes it more difficult for people to take your leadership seriously.

Identifying Behaviors - Extremely cooperative with little to no assertiveness throughout the conversation.

2.   Avoiding (I Lose – You Lose)

Ever want to skip the negotiation altogether and just hope things turn out for the better? That's what the tendency is with the avoiding negotiation style. People who may use this style of negotiating don't like to engage in conflict and are good at ignoring/side-stepping issues. To address issues of conflict when engaged in this style you must be direct about the issues. It may be helpful to bring in a third party to keep the conversation moving toward a resolution.

Those who engage in the avoiding style of negotiation should be aware that resentment can creep up after the deal is done because the result of the negotiation is one-sided.

Women who want to avoid disagreements or those who place a high value on the opinions of others can fall into the style of avoiding negotiations. This can be beneficial in some circumstances, however, as a leader, learning how to manage conflict is a skill that must be gained in order to drive results for the organization.

Identifying Behaviors- Avoiding the issues, postponing or canceling meetings, changing topics to avoid discussing the hard stuff.

3.   Collaborating (I Win – You Win)

Look at the issue(s) at hand with the viewpoint of determining how we both get what we want and walk away feeling good. Negotiation is an exchange of value that implies that each party has something that the other wants or needs. Asking open-ended questions which can't be answered with a simple yes or no opens the door to find creative solutions to reach a deal based on the common goal of exchanging value.

In salary negotiation and business deals, using a collaborative approach in negotiation maintains both reputation and relationship. If an employer gets the upper hand on a new employee during the salary negotiation process, the employee may find out later and share how unfairly she's been treated. Company's hire talent because there is a function that requires a person with a particular skill set to fill that role. The cost to hire and train a new employee can be tens of thousands of dollars so it is in the best financial interest for the company to give a potential new employee a good deal. But, remember without proper research a potential employee doesn't know if she's getting a good deal or a great deal and that's why it is essential to conduct research prior to accepting a job offer. Even with the collaborative negotiation approach, without the facts it is hard to distinguish between a good deal and a great deal.

Identifying Behaviors - Conversation driven based on mutual benefits and a focus on maintaining long-term relationship(s).

4.   Competing (I win – You lose)

The competing style of negotiation focused on one-sided outcomes. Think of a person trying to get as much as they can at your expense. The person who engages in this style will try to exploit areas that are most important to you so that they get more of what they want. If you find yourself speaking more than the other party or if they're asking for detailed information without sharing information with you, take a step back to ensure you're not providing details that will be used against you to the other party's benefit.

When the negotiation is moving at a fast-pace, it is a sign that one party may be pushing the process at an accelerated speed as a power play to claim more upfront and get the deal done. When two parties engage in the competing style, it can end up in an impasse. An impasse is a point in which the negotiation can't move forward; this is also referred to as gridlock.

Identifying Behaviors - Assertive behavior that focused on the deal and self-confident throughout the conversation.

5.   Compromising (I Lose / Win Some – You Lose/ Win Some)

This negotiation style is best used among two parties that have a relationship and a foundation of trust. Neither party actually gets what they want from the other. There can be numerous causes for this type of approach but often times the parties don't have or want to invest them time to thoroughly address each issue on the table. If this style is used too often, it can give the impression that one is not prepared, and others can take advantage of the lack of preparation and trust. When using this style of negotiation, remember that "winging it" may get you a good deal, but it may leave you a few inches away from a great deal.

The overarching theme in this book is the win/win negotiation approach which is classified as the collaborating style. However, even with the sense of collaborative negotiation, build a strategy that is a mix of these styles so that your most confident version of self shows up at the negotiation table. Negotiation is not a one size fits all approach. What works in one negotiation may need to be switched up for the next negotiation even with the same party. This is a muscle. The more you practice negotiating the stronger the skill will become and you'll be able to navigate the conversation so that you don't leave any money on the table.

Listening for details

> "Whoever answers before listening is both foolish and shameful."
> *-Proverbs 18:13*

We just covered the five types of negotiation styles but I'm going to add a sixth to the list. That's the listening strategy. There are proverbs and quotes that underscore the importance of listening more than one speaks and the popularity of this theory is true for numerous reasons. These are the benefits of listening more than you speak in a negotiation.

- Gain insight into what isn't being discussed

- Ability to notice body language that may provide valuable details into the counterparts thought process

- Avoid oversharing too much information that may be disadvantageous to you

- Avoid confusing the counterpart by providing irrelevant information

Listening is a skill that we'll talk more about in other chapters of the book. It's a critical component to negotiating win/win deals as well as being able to distinguish between a good deal and a great deal. Start paying attention to your natural tendencies in negotiations, and gradually begin to assess your daily conversations to help you determine which negotiation style(s) you gravitate towards the most. As you build the negotiation muscle, you can begin to assess the negotiation style(s) of the people you communicate with the most. The caution in trying to determine someone else's negotiation style upfront is that you may confirm bias or make assumptions which can impact the fact of that person's personality or their tactic in negotiation. It is possible to mix negotiation styles as well as change a style even in the midst of a negotiation. Don't get married to a style, assess the situation of each negotiation and the person(s) you're negotiating with so that you're setting yourself to present the request and make a decision without leaving money on the table. This chapter is the shortest in the book by design; the five styles are impactful and useful to understand. Reflection and self-awareness are two powerful tools to engage as you maximize this chapter.

Reading through the initial descriptions which negotiation style do you most relate to at this time?

LATTE - Negotiation Strategy

> Though it seems curious, I do not remember ever asking for anything but what I got it. And I always received it as an answer to my prayers. ~ *Sojourner Truth*

There is an art to preparing for a negotiation and developing your strategy. If you don't ask for what you want, the chances of you getting that which is in your mind is limited. You've got to be savvy in your request and present those requests confidently. Although no two negotiations are the same, each negotiation requires dedicated attention to the factors that are important to all the negotiating parties. The goal is not to get a good deal but a great deal and a strong reputation that will lead others to say that they will want to do business with you again. There are numerous ways to prepare for a negotiation, but in this section, we're going to explore the "LATTE" method, a negotiation framework that I've used to help numerous win, lock in big business deals, and compensation packages. As a self-professed latte lover, I drink at least one of these espresso beverages a day. Just as it is my daily routine and part of my fuel to consume this beverage, it's also a metaphor to reflect on using the LATTE method daily. Each time a plane takes flight, a pilot and co-pilot engage in completing a pre-flight checklist. The purpose of the pre-flight checklist is to ensure each step of safety precaution is taken to ensure the smoothest flight possible. Think of the LATTE method as your negotiation checklist, your safety measure so that you ensure you've covered the basics to prepare to make a confident ask and well-informed decision. LATTE is a five-part negotiation strategy framework, and the acronym stands for: Look at the details, Anticipate Challenges, Think about your walk away point, Talk it through, and Evaluate options.

The LATTE method is great for negotiating, as its core negotiation is problem solving. In any situation where there is a problem to be solved, you can engage with a latte method. Think of the leading teams that are resolving conflict in your professional or personal life. By using the five-step framework outlined below, the LATTE method encourages you to think about the situation fully and from an objective manner. Problem solving often times can induce stress, and with stress, the ability to cloud judgment because of heightened emotions. What the LATTE method does is engage analysis of the circumstances. It increases your leadership skills by promoting clarity in thought process, thus pulling on all facts to look through the entire situation. Leverage the LATTE method in creating a strategy that pulls upon all available information so that the best decision can be made in the moment.

Look at the details

"The more you know, the better informed decision you will be able to make" ~ *Jacqueline V. Twillie*

80% of a negotiation is done in the preparation. Before you get to the nitty gritty of making a request or deciding if an offer is great, take time to analyze the details. Prior to any negotiation, spend time looking at the details from your perspective and the other party's perspective. Put yourself in the shoes of the person you're having a conversation with as well so that as you prepare, you're looking at the full scope of the details related to the negotiation. This is a good time to remind you that a negotiation is just a conversation, it's not a battle. A practical rule of thumb that I've shared with many of my clients has just been 1 hour of preparation per $10,000. For instance, if you are negotiating an $80,000 salary, spend 8 hours in preparation. Likewise, if you're negotiating a $60,000 business, still spend six hours. This may seem like a lot of time, but if it's a difference between $5,000 or $20,000, you'd rather spend that time versus not having the money or leaving money on the table. As you prepare for the negotiation, a few things to keep in mind are:

- **Market Rate**

The market rate is what someone gets paid with your experience and educational background and your specific geographic area. An operations manager in Dallas Texas may earn a significantly different salary from a manager with similar duties in the same company but located in Tampa Florida or New York City. Using on-line salary calculators, such as PayScale, Glassdoor, and LinkedIn salary, are great places to start. However, the online data does not disclose how many people's salary data is averaged, their gender, how long they've been at the company, and how old the data is. All those factors matter because markets change. Industries change and demands on skills change, so depending on the economy and many other factors, the age of the data can be irrele-vant to what the current market rate is. Therefore, use the online figures as a starting place for your research. This is where tapping into your network comes in really handy. Statistically, men earn on average more than women in almost every industry. When you're seeking advice on what the market rate is, speak with white men who are the highest earners in most industries. Customize the be-low example when you're having the conversation sur-rounding market-rate, digging into the factors to help you assess what salary range you should ask for.

"Hi, John. Are you available to speak with me next week? I would like to get your opinion on a salary range. I'm potential-ly exploring new career opportunities."

Once a face-to-face meeting or phone call is scheduled, review your online data so that you're making the best use of time allotted.

"John, thanks for meeting with me. I really value your opinion. As I mentioned before, I'm exploring career op-portunities, and I'd like to get a better understanding of the type of salary that I should expect for a person with my experience in this field. I pulled some online data, and from what I've learned, I should expect somewhere between the high 80s mid 90s base salary. Does that sound about right to you?"

Once you asked the question, do not over explain by

providing all the details of how you gathered the data. Remember, this person is lending you time to share advice; therefore, give the person an opportunity to give you their opinion. This is a great time to take notes.

Generally, when this question is presented to someone who is knowledgeable about the industry and the geographic area, they will say one of these options.

- Yes, that sounds about right

- No, that's a little high for someone with your experience

- No, that's a bit low for someone with your experience

- Yes, and...

With the information that you gather from the in-person or phone call meeting, you'll be better prepared to answer the question when a recruiter or hiring manager asks you what your salary expectations are.

It's a good idea to start these conversations prior to fully engaging in a job search and to have at least three people give you feedback. The purpose of this exercise is to verify by fact checking the online salary data that you found. Beyond salary seek to gain insight into:

- Industry Perks

- Trends within Industry

- Unique skills that you bring to the company

Prepare for a job interview by gaining information on the organization and the people you'll be speaking with, use the same framework when preparing for the career related negotiations. Pilots are required to use a checklist before they fly a plane. It doesn't matter how many years of experience or how many times that day they had flown, they still have to use a checklist, and the importance of using the checklist is so that they don't miss any critical areas. At the end of this book, you'll find several negotiation checklists that you can use for a number of different negotiations. It's important that you use these checklists no matter how many times you've negotiated with the same parties, because preparation is the key to setting yourself up for success. The more information you have in a negotiation the better prepared you are to make well-informed decisions. If there are areas that you are not familiar with that you anticipate may come up in the negotiations, spend a considerable amount of time researching that area so that you are not caught off guard when it comes up in the conversation.

Leaders and business owners who are looking at the details want to consider all of the factors that provide the most accurate information available. Whether you have an assistant pulling information for you or you're doing the research for yourself, thoroughly review all the information that is available. Couple online research with talking to people, with knowledge about the person, company, and additional parties related to a negotiation. If possible, rely on at least three sources of data to ensure you're expanding your frame of reference and pulling in information that might not have come up in your initial thought process of reviewing details.

Anticipate Challenges

"Don't limit yourself. Many people limit themselves to what they think they can do. You can go as far as your mind lets you. What you believe, remember, you can achieve."
~Mary Kay Ash

When preparing for a negotiation, it can be helpful to write an outline of the issues that are important to you, as well as anticipate what the other party may say in response to your request. When thinking of the other party's response, formulate how you will address each point without discrediting them and also acknowledging that they may have a valid point. This can be a form of putting yourself in the other person's shoes. Once you drafted an outline of your request and inserted the anticipated response from the other party, conduct a roleplay simulation. Prior to engaging in a roleplay, turn on an audio or video recording device, and at the end of the role play, conduct an honest assessment of how you delivered your message. When conducting the assessment, use the following points to gauge your performance.

- Tone of voice

- Rate of speech

- Use of fillers such as um, ah, so, you know

- Ratio of how you spoke vs listened

- Summarizing of points to clarify understanding

- Ability to let the other party finish his statement without cutting them off

- Articulating your point without repeating yourself

Do not skip on topics that you are uncomfortable with or a topic that you hope will not come up. Identify your own blind spot and the areas that you aren't as strong in, and formulate a strategy so that you don't disclose those areas that can be used as leverage against you later in the negotiation. One of the intended purposes of anticipating challenges is that you are not caught off guard with information related to your negotiation. In business, the more information you have the better informed decisions you can make.

Research the market rate each time you negotiate, even if you've negotiated what seems to be the same details as before. The market rate is defined as the wages a person earns with a stated experience level, within a defined geographic area, and specific to a particular title. Recommended sites are PayScale, Paysa, or Glassdoor to equip you with this salary information. Once researching the market rate online, take it a step further and verify those numbers by speaking with someone who is well-versed in your industry about market rate. By speaking with people that are within your industry, you will be able to gauge whether your expectation for the market is realistic. Requesting and sharing this level of detail should only be done with a trusted colleague within your industry. For many people, discussing money, even a market rate can be taboo; therefore, using your best professional judgement as to who you have this conversation with is important to having a meaningful dialogue. Within the conversation, share the amount you plan to ask for, as well as the lowest amount you will accept. The right person should provide insight on whether your expectation is on, above, or below market rate. As a result, you'll walk away from the conversation armed with this knowledge that you will know if you are getting a good or bad deal as it relates to the market rate.

Think about your walk away point

> "Strengthen your decision making by considering at what point you have to walk way."
> ~ *Jacqueline V. Twillie*

Research shows that having options strengthens one's ability to walk away from a negotiation if necessary. Set the parameters in which you will walk away from a discussion before it begins. By doing so, you reduce the chances of responding emotionally instead of factually to the deal that is presented. Emotions are normal in negotiations and it's okay to feel whatever you feel. However, you should not make any decisions while you are in a heightened emotional state. Self-awareness of rising emotions will help you to take a break or slow down a negotiation so that you can think clearly and make a decision based on facts instead of feelings.

In the process of establishing what you would like to get out of the deal, think of the areas that you're willing to compromise based on what you know about the other party. Use the negotiation checklist which is included in the back of this book when establishing your desires as well as your walk away point. Female negotiators often set lower goals in negotiation as compared to male negotiators when preparing the list of things you would like to achieve from the negotiation. Start with a good list and then on the second draft create a list of higher aspirations. This will force you to think bigger and build higher expectations for the negotiation. Margaret Neele, a professor at Stanford University, says, "expectation drives behavior in negotiation."

Set big goals within negotiations. Based on the information that you find about what you can expect realistically, shoot for the high end of the range, not just the bare minimum that you need. A great resource to expand your thinking in terms of setting big goals in negotiation is a book called mindset by Carol Dweck. By aiming for the high end of the range as respiration, the language that you use in how you communicate to the other party will focus on that versus the low end. Your goals should be realistic, and in some cases, realistic but ambitious enough to stretch you which may make you feel uncomfortable. One factor that often prevents women from thinking about large negotiation goals is a question such as am I good enough or do I deserve this? Those questions are what Carol Dweck calls a fixed mindset and can be symptoms of the imposter syndrome. We'll talk about imposter syndrome later in the book. If you notice that you're stuck and can't think large in terms of your expectations for the negotiation engage with a trusted mentor or coach to help you think of achieving big goals. Negotiation can be a win-win for both parties. You can get the best, and the other person can get the best at the same time. It's a matter of understanding the exchange of value and owning the value that you bring to the table.

As you evaluate the areas that you're willing to give in on, think about the value that you add to the other party. What you give in on, should not reduce the value that you're adding. The walk away point will be when the value you add and the value you receive are imbalanced in the other party's favor.

Talk it through

"I feel that luck is preparation meeting opportunity."
~ Oprah Winfrey

It's been stated before and is worth restating that negotiation is just a conversation; it is not a battle. When you present your request, remember to be confident in your tone of voice and body language, even if you're communicating over the phone. Talk through what you want to say using an outline and carefully thinking of what you want to share along with the purpose of sharing such information. Similarly consider the questions you may want to ask as well as the intention behind each question. A helpful tip in talking it through is using the cell phone to practice what you want to say in advance and then listening to the recording so that you understand how you sound before you walk into the conversation. In an earlier chapter, avoiding backlash was covered during the phase of talking it through. Let's go deeper into that area. Sometimes asking for items one-by-one can come off as unprepared. To avoid that perception, present your request in a bundle or package, then get into the details of each item.

How to ask for what you want in a package format - Don't negotiate issue by issue; package your request together so you don't sound greedy or ungrateful. I know you may be thinking that men don't have to worry about this characterization, and in some cases, you may be right. Our goal in successfully negotiating is not to sound like men; it's to get the best deal available to us. Some women think it is easier to negotiate for one item at a time, for instance, salary, then flexible work schedule arrangements, then tuition reimbursement. The problem with this type of strategy is that after coming to an agreement on one issue, and you go back to the negotiating table, it appears that you are just trying to get more because you got the first request or that because you did not get the first request you're trying to get more. In either case, whether you received your first request or not, going back to ask for more proves to be ineffective. For example, if you're asking for a delayed start date, an increase in base salary, and additional vacation time, share those three issues upfront then discuss the details of each.

Confidence boosting tips before an interview whether in-person or via phone.

- Follow-up your favorite morning ritual that gets you in a great mood

- Wear your favorite outfit

- Create a playlist with music that pumps you up

- Remember, you can only control what you can control, so don't sweat the small stuff

Prior to the conversation, review important facts and have a document that you can reference with easily identifiable key points. Bring this to the conversation if appropriate. Practice what you want to say aloud and upon reflection consider revising your expectations. If during the process of talking it through you uncover additional questions that you did not uncover when looking at the details, take a step back and gather additional details. From that, you can reset any expectations whether it is to expand or pull back on what you previously thought. Avoid making assumptions by pulling as many facts as possible. Use talking it through as a phase to boost your confidence and become familiar with the facts in speaking confidently about such.

Evaluate options

> "As a freelancer, as a writer, and running my company, people have always tried to negotiate me down. Some might think that I might accept their offers because they think I don't have many options. The truth is, I always have options available to me." ~ *Luvvie Ajayi*

Congratulations on receiving an offer. It's an exciting moment in the process of searching for a job. Generally, the job offer will be extended verbally via a phone call before a formal letter is sent. Offer letters are usually attached in an email from an HR professional within the organization that has extended the offer. In the initial moment of excitement, express enthusiasm for receiving the offer but do not say yes until you have read all of the conditions and the letter.

How to say it:

"Thank you for extending the offer. I'm excited, and I know that I can add significant value to the organization. I would like to review the written offer and will get back with you in two or three business days with any questions that I may have as well with the formal acceptance. I look forward to moving along in this process."

By holding off on accepting the verbal offer without seeing the written offer, you increase your leverage to negotiate for a higher salary, additional vacation days, a higher 401K match, or any other important items. If you accept too soon, it becomes more challenging and awkward to negotiate after you have verbally committed.

Once you receive an offer, refer back to the parameters you set for walking away. It's also important to remember not to put your feelings over the facts in this stage. Before accepting, countering, or declining an offer, review the written offer more than once. It may help to review, then take a few hours to process before reviewing the written offer again. A common flaw in salary negotiation is that the candidate will accept the offer before seeing the written offer or accepting an offer with verbal conditions that are not formally recorded for the company to have a knowledge of what was agreed upon with two parties, presumably you and the person who extended the offer.

ASK!

> Don't ask for permission to negotiate, just negotiate.
> ~ *Jacqueline V. Twillie*

Women are less likely to initiate negotiations as compared to their male counterparts. It's true in professional and personal situations where women tend to second guess if they should make a request and put significant weight on how others will view them for asking. It is valid to be aware of how the request will be perceived; however, it best serves women to use that concern as a tool to overcome bias and present the request in a manner that is non-alarming to the other party. Negotiation is a muscle; the more it used the stronger that skill becomes. When one struggles with overcoming fear to ask, start by negotiating small issues that don't carry as much anxiety.

Exercise: 'Consider calling companies that you do business with and asking for a discount. Small savings related to recurring monthly bills like cable, cell phone, or renters insurance can add up to a significant saving and put more money in your pocket.

This is a sample script that you can customize to your situation. First, find the contact number of the customer service department, then find a time in your schedule that will allow you to wait on hold for 30 minutes or so.

Once you get someone on the phone, try this.

"Am I getting the best possible rate?" That's it, then pause and wait for an answer. Do not dive into an explanation. Track your success and let us know how it goes.

Anchor - Negotiators often try to introduce a reference point or "Anchor" early in a negotiation. This reference point becomes the basis for counter offers and demands. Setting an anchor point close to your desired outcome sometimes helps modify the expectations of the other party.

There's a phrase common among those who teach children that says, "if at first you don't succeed, try, try again." This concept can also be applied to negotiation with an addition. If you don't succeed, ask what I or we can do differently to reach agreement?

Prior to engaging in the conversation where the request is presented, create an outline that includes what you want to achieve from the negotiation and the points that are of importance. Be specific about what you want and the value you offer— in exchange for what you want.

Follow that step with a dedicated time to conduct research all issues and people, no detail is too small. The more you know about the issues on the table, the better prepared you will be, and that confidence will be visible to the person(s) you are negotiating with. Overcoming bias in negotiating is done by understanding the issues but also the styles of the other party. Avoid the common trap of viewing the outline as a wish list that will be easy to achieve. Issues may sound great from your perspective but do not be blinded by your own great ideas, put yourself in their shoes to be prepared for opposing views. During this exercise, look for ways to add more value instead of offering a lower rate, discount, or accepting a lower salary. If you encounter a situation where you are at an impasse on money, think outside of the box.

What's an impasse? An impasse is a point in the negotiation where the parties do not agree and have reached a stopping point. Typically in this situation, the conversation stops and each party digs into their position with no willingness to compromise on their key issue(s). In salary negotiation, an impasse is often encountered on the issue of money. A few methods of moving past the impasse is to get a third party or mediator involved to be a neutral voice, potentially involving a hiring manager instead of the hiring recruiter. An impasse is not always a bad thing for salary negotiation

Justify your request by sharing your track record of success related to the negotiation issues. Facts over feelings will win in negotiations.

Sometimes, you are presented with a deal that is not in your favor. Do not spend time and energy on a deal that is not in your best interest.

When you accepted a job, you may or may not have negotiated your compensation package, and while you should always negotiate the best deal for you based on the market rate, also consider factors that will help you meet your objectives. What things will set you up for success in the current or new role?

- New equipment or software to increase productivity and efficiency

- Budget to attend a conference or receive a certification - stay ahead of the competition

- Office space - if your work requires you to handle confidential information you may want to ask for a room with a door or an open cubicle

- New title - it may help you get your foot in the door with a new client or show your internal company customers that you have authority to make decisions and prompt them to give you more respect

This list could go on and on. I encourage you to think about everything you need to achieve success in your role and then strategize how to ask for those things so that your employer understands that giving you what you want is to their benefit.

Create a list of items or tools that you may need to be effective in your role.

Timing matters. If there are any events that negatively impact the mood of the other party, offer to postpone the negotiation. When having a conversation and the stakes are high, awareness of the right time can be the difference between a good deal and a great deal. For instance, if someone has experienced a life-altering event, there is a fire drill, or some other matter of critical importance, do not force a schedule to stay on track. It's better to pause and regroup at a time when factors that may influence the negotiation are not as hectic.

If a negotiation is taking place and you recognize that the other party is impacted by factors beyond your control, stay focused as the conversation flows naturally. Look for ways to slow the conversation or pause it until a later date. It is advantageous to hold off until the timing is in your favor.

Overcoming Fear

> "When I dare to be powerful - to use my strength in the service of my vision, then it becomes less and less important whether I am afraid."

> ~ *Audre Lorde*

Over the year of coaching women to negotiate business deals and salaries, there is one word that is a consistent reason for not asking for more. That reason is FEAR. Fear of not knowing what to say, how to say it, or what the response will be. When we place the facts over the concerns of fear, the stats are startling. Women who don't negotiate, starting with their first professional job, stand to lose over $500,000 over the course of their career according to the book, Women Don't Ask. A factor that should be considered each time fear creeps up is what is it going to cost me to NOT ask? What are you giving up in exchange for the comfort of not having that conversation? Brene' Brown, best-selling author and researcher, says that we should "choose discomfort over resentment." In other words, be uncomfortable briefly in discussing money, rather than being comfortable in that moment and later regret not asking and more painfully not having the money that someone with your experience and expertise should be earning. The first step in overcoming fear to ask for more is confronting all the issues that make you second-guess yourself and your ability to ask for more.

What prevented you from asking in the past?

TURN YOUR FEARS INTO AFFIRMATIONS:

An exercise in overcoming fear to present your request in negotiation is creating affirmations that tackle the fear head on.

Here's an example: If your fear is, "I don't deserve to be paid the market rate because I don't meet all of the qualifications on the job description," flip it and write it in reverse.

I deserve to be paid the market rate because my skills and experience have prepared me to bring exceptional value to this role and to exceed expectations and deliver results.

For each fear that you have surrounding presenting your request in the negotiation, create a positive affirmation to help you overcome it and review that several times, especially when to get deep into thought about reasons why you shouldn't ask or when doubting your skills.

Power Moves

> "It took me quite a long time to develop a voice, and now that I have it, I am not going to be silent."
> - *Madeleine Albright*

Active listening is a way of listening and responding to another person that improves mutual understanding. Often when people talk to each other, they don't listen attentively. We are often distracted, half listening, half thinking about something else. Failing to gain insight or details due to lack of listening is a common way to give up power. In business, life, and in negotiations, information is power; the more information you have, the better informed decisions you are able to make. Building the skill of strategic listening is a power move that when mastered is a game changer in all forms of communication. It is a skill that enhances leadership effectiveness.

9 Ways to boost your active listening skills

1. Face the speaker or listen without multitasking on an electronic device

2. Maintain eye contact through the conversation

3. Be attentive, but relaxed

4. Keep an open mind especially if you have opposing views or ideas on the matter

5. Listen to the words and body language

6. Don't interrupt even if you feel you can passionate about the topic

7. Don't impose your "solutions." prematurely

8. Don't text or email during the conversation

9. Repeat what was said in a natural manner to confirm understanding

Repeat positive phrases the other party mentioned as to why they want you to be a part of the team. Express why you want to work with or for the other party with a keen focus on your common goals.

If the conversation gets off track, what phrases can you use to get back to the points you want to cover during the negotiation? STAY POSITIVE! Keep the focus on how you can add value and reach the objectives discussed.

Negotiating Salary

The Offer &
Counter Offer

A job offer is presented at the conclusion of the interview process. While the entire interview process is a part of the negotiation of the terms of employment and compensation, do not begin until the offer has been presented to the candidate from the potential employer. As a job candidate going through the interview process, asking open-ended questions throughout each stage of the interview gives the candidate an insight into how the company operates and how badly they need a person to fill the vacant position. By gathering data through the process of asking questions that cannot be answered with a simple yes or no - it provides leverage to negotiate for a mutually beneficial job package.

Most companies do expect the new employee to negotiate, and for that reason, the first offer is rarely the best offer. The company will come in lower than what they can actually pay. The first offer is typically within the range of the market rate for someone with similar experience in that geographic area earns. However, there may be additional benefits and perks that are not included in the initial offer that the candidate may not know about if there isn't communication with people who know the industry or company well. The key to uncovering the full range of benefits and perks is to tap into your professional network to find out what top candidates are offered.

Many women do not counter an offer for numerous reasons. Here are the most common reasons why women leave money on the table:

- Don't know that offer can be countered

- Fear that countering will make the company pull the offer

- Not sure what to say and how to say or when to say they want more

- Desperation that the current employment situation is bleak, so something is better than nothing

- Worried that they won't be liked

- Fear that asking will make her look greedy

- Fear that whatever the counter will be "too much"

This list could go on and on. There are no shortage of reasons why women don't ask for more when they receive an offer, but the cost of negotiating is far greater than the discomfort of presenting a counter offer. But there is good news, research shows that when a job description states that the salary in negotiable that women negotiate at the same rate as men.

As a candidate, you will typically get a verbal offer before you receive a written offer. The offer isn't real until you receive it in a written format. Generally this will be a document attached within an email. Excitement is a common emotion when a job offer is extended; however, don't let feelings trump the facts of the moment. Before committing to or declining an offer, express enthusiasm so that the company knows you are seriously interested, ask when you can expect to see the offer in writing, followed with clarity on the timeline for your response. An offer is not real until you see it in black and white. The core of the counter is not about being greedy. It is about reaching a mutually beneficial deal that compensates you well in exchange for the work you will perform.

The core of the counteroffer comes to two points.

1. What is the target?

2. What is the walk away point?

Before you fire off an email or send a text to counter, consider the two main points from a long-term viewpoint. You may be tempted to avoid the awkwardness of negotiating over the phone and want to embrace sending an email instead, but there is value in making a phone call to start the counter offer conversation. The counteroffer process takes time and may involve multiple parties on the employer's side, so don't expect a final answer right away. As a result of the number of people involved in the process, you'll want to get a gauge on your initial request and that's best done over the phone. If you go right to email, you may have to wait several days to hear anything, and during the waiting period, anxiety can arise and you'll be tempted to send another message and cave without allowing them to reply to your counter request.

 If you need a reason to be brave and have the hard conversation over the phone, consider that the base salary that you'll accept will impact any bonuses, step raises, and retirement matches. Therefore, with the facts in mind, consider the counteroffer as a revised version of the initial offer that makes it more desirable for you to accept the offer. Framing the counter offer in this way is of benefit to women because it knocks out the common hurdles that prevent women from asking and leaving money on the table. This type of offer permits a person to decline a previous offer and allows offer negotiations to continue. Do not forget that negotiation is a conversation, not a battle! During the preparation phase, you've gathered lots of information from the market rates to the items that will make you most successful in the role. As the conversation flows naturally, use the information you gather from asking open-ended questions to build a stronger case for what you want. Leverage is defined as the use of something to build maximum advantage.

leverage

/ˈlev(ə)rij/

verb

1. use (something) to maximum advantage.

"the organization needs to leverage its key resources"

By taking copious notes throughout the interview process, you'll be able to pull facts that support why you're worth being paid at the top of the market rate for the position that you've been offered. A few things to consider are:

- How long the position has been vacant

- How quickly they need someone to fill the role

- Why this role is vital to larger company/organizational goals

- Specific reasons why they think you're the "right" woman for the role

- What they'll want to address first as a new member of the team

When leveraging the information you've gathered, keep in mind that this is a win/win opportunity. The organization needs someone and you want to be paid at the top of the range for completing the work and helping the company to reach and exceed goals. Therefore, at the beginning of the counter, express genuine enthusiasm for the offer as well as express how you are confident you'll be an asset to the organization.

Consider how your target salary and walk away point falls within the market rate for the position in comparison to the total dollar value of the offer, including benefits.

Target Rate=	
Walk Away Rate=	
Market Rate =	
Total Dollar Value Package =	

Make a list of the areas that are most important to you

in addition to salary and rank them in order of importance to you. You'll want to start the request by packaging your request together instead of listing each issue separately, waiting for a response for one before mentioning the other. Here's an example of how the counter offer conversation could start:

"Thank you for this offer. I'm excited to move forward in this process. I'm eager to become a member of the team and contribute. There are a few things I'd like to discuss, the base salary, signing bonus, start date, and vacation days. Based on my research, the base salary for someone with my level of experience is $XXX (insert salary) and the average signing bonus is $XXX. Is there flexibility in those areas?"

Pause here and wait for a response.

You may be tempted to over talk and provide an in-depth rationale about your request, but it's best to stick to the facts and be concise. You want to find out if there is any objection before you attempt to address the objection. Consider a moment when you were in a store ready to make a purchase and the sales associate kept talking and telling you about the features long after you had decided you were going to make the purchase. How did you feel? If you're like me, you probably got a little annoyed or decided to leave the store without making the purchase. By over talking after presenting your request for the counter offer, you could have the same affect. Be confident and concise, then wait for a response. After you've given time for the other party to respond naturally, move the conversation to the other request.

"Ok, I'll look forward to you getting back to me on the base salary and bonus. In my current role, I receive 28 days vacation. The offer letter referenced 22 days. Is there wiggle room on the paid vacation time?"

"Ok, lastly from the list, I mentioned earlier the start date is fairly quick. I'll need to give my current employer notice and bring my projects to a close in the offer letter you requested to start on the 2nd of the month. I'm wondering if we could push that back to the 11th?"

The person you're negotiating with may need to get additional approval for your request, so before wrapping up the phone conversation, ask for the next steps timeline. By asking for the timeline, it can reduce any anxiety caused by waiting for a response. Some employers get back to the candidate quickly while others may stall the timeline for one reason or another. During the waiting period, do not second guess yourself because if you don't ask or didn't ask the answer would be no. Wait it out by keeping yourself busy with other tasks or by communicating with your negotiation strategist/career coach.

A few points to consider prior to engaging in a counter offer conversation.

- Do not ask for permission to counter offer. Present your request confidently based on the value you know you can deliver.

- Do not apologize for countering. Women who apologize for asking, give away their leverage and are less likely to be taken seriously. Be polite but firm in your request.

- Facts over feelings. Don't get too emotional about your employment circumstances that you fail to think objectively.

- Do not lie; lies come back to haunt the candidate and could cause early termination with the new employer if found out.

- Do not bluff without real options. It is unwise to

tell the employer that you have other offers if you don't have other offers on the table. It's ok to use the other facts you've gathered for leverage. Industries are small and people talk; it will be easy for the employer to find out what another company is offering.

- Don't throw in the towel because you are anxious and tired of waiting. By staying calm and waiting for the other party to respond, you show them that you know your value and are worth being paid top dollar.

- Be prepared to walk away if the company comes back and they cannot come close to paying your target. If it is at or below your walk away point be firm and walk away.

- Knowing your value is more than asking for more money; it is also having the courage to walk away from a deal that isn't aligned with your realistic salary and benefits expectations.

- Don't bring up personal financial obligations such as mortgage, property taxes, car repairs, student loans, etc... The counter should be based on data for what the market pays. Don't discuss your personal financial wish list.

- Be professional but concise. When countering, you want to avoid oversharing any information that could weaken your position for the request. For instance, if they know you're going to accept the offer no matter what, they're less likely to find the resources to accommodate the counter.

- If you hear "no" during negotiation it's okay, and part of the process, don't freak out. Remain composed, and if appropriate, ask open ended follow-up questions. We'll cover more on this in the "No" section of the book.

- Don't burn any bridges if things don't go as you'd like them to. Remember that the world is small, and it's better to bow out gracefully than cause a ruckus.

- Be confident in the value you will bring to the organization.

Accepting the offer

Congratulations, you have the offer you want. But wait, don't just flat out accept it, even if it sounds great and you're really excited. Always ask for an opportunity to review everything in writing–but express enthusiasm so that they know that you're interested. The money might sound good at first glance, but when you look at benefits like healthcare, you may find the coverage is less than you anticipated; if so, you may want to negotiate a better salary. Ask for a few days to review the details of the offer in writing. This gives you the opportunity to think clearly once the excitement of the offer settles down and you were able to think clearly about the entire compensation package. Refer to the latte method to ensure you're considering all factors before the formal acceptance. Keep in mind that if it isn't in writing, there is no guarantee that you're going to get something that was discussed verbally. Even though the person may assure you verbally, request that some written record of those verbal agreements are included so that you have something to reference back to and to ensure that you are not leaving money or other benefits on the table. Sometimes with people who have great intentions to follow through on verbal offers, something comes up whether expected or unexpected, that may force them to take time off of work or even leave the company, leaving you to have no leverage to claim the things that were in the verbal agreement which underscores the importance of getting everything in a written format.

It's much harder to come back and negotiate after you've already accepted a verbal offer. Therefore, resist the urge to accept in the initial moments to say yes. While reviewing the written offer, look at the details of what was discussed verbally and have a trusted mentor or advisor give the offer a second look. It can be easy to miss small details in the initial moments of excitement. Oftentimes women are concerned about politeness and think that it is rude to ask for time to review the documents. It is not rude to ask for time to review a written offer. It speaks to your leadership ability to be able to ask questions and have time to analyze details before making a final decision. In an instance similar to this, it increases the level of respect that you have for yourself as well as how others view you, which is more important than the concern of whether someone likes you more or less because you've asked for time to see a written document and review it carefully. Consider the job that you're being hired to do and how it reflects upon you to have a keen attention to detail.

If there are any items that were discussed verbally that are not in the written offer, ask if it was left out unintentionally and what would need to happen to include that in the written offer. Be concise with the questions and clear on how you communicate any items that need to be included. Given that you've probably spoken to the person you're negotiating with several times, there's no need to go into extensive detail as you should both have an understanding of what was discussed and what needs to be added. Allow for a few days for updates to be made. Wait until you have the written updates before signing an agreement. If for some reason there is resistance to including in the written offer things that were discussed verbally, it's time to pause as this is a significant red flag in terms of being able to trust that the other party will deliver what they said they would do. Engage the conversation using open-ended questions to get a deeper understanding of the hesitation before making a decision, especially if your initial reaction may be to walk away. Stephen Covey once said, "Seek first to understand then be understood." This phrase rings true in a situation where there is a slowdown in a negotiation because a written offer doesn't reflect the verbal offer.

Salary Too Low?

Express your desire to move forward and your ability to do the job well. However, in order to reach the agreement, you will need the following in order to effectively do the job.

NEVER GIVE AN ULTIMATUM!

If you don't want to move forward, gracefully decline. It's a small world, do not burn any bridges.

Say: I'm really excited to receive this offer. I know that I can add significant value to the organization. However, the salary is below the market rate. What can <u>we</u> do about that?

Pause, do not over explain why you are asking this question.

If they need to speak with someone else,

Ask: *When will you be able to speak with that person, and when can I expect to hear back from you?*

Pause, do not over explain why you are asking this question.

- *If they say, there is nothing we can do,*

Ask: *Have any exceptions ever been made?*

Pause, do not over explain why you are asking this question.

Follow up based on what they share. The key here is to listen for what they say and what they do not say.

Pause 2-3 seconds before responding.

- If they won't budge on the money,

Ask: *Under which scenario would we be able to move me up to market rate if I accept this salary?*

Pause, be concise and avoid oversharing.

Follow up question: Can we review my performance in 60 days and develop a written plan to adjust the salary to market rate during the 60-day time period?

Pause, do not over explain why you are asking this question.

When you receive more than one offer:

Be honest, don't ever try this strategy if you don't have multiple offers.

Say: As you know, I've been interviewing for other positions. I have received another offer for money. *Share how you will add value to the company you want to work for the most and explain your #1 reason for wanting to work with this company.*

What will you say:

Turning Down The Offer

Say: Thank you for the offer, but after much consideration I have made the difficult decision to go another direction. Thank you again for this opportunity. **Follow- up with a brief written statement**

Signing Bonus

According to a 2016 World At Work survey, over 76% of participants noted they received a signing bonus. This type of bonus is not just reserved for C-Suite executives. Negotiating a signing bonus is more common among top executives. For some, a signing bonus can be in the $50,000 range; however, most mid-career professionals will see a signing bonus between $5,000 to $10,000. Most signing bonuses are based on a percentage of the base salary. Typically the bonus will fall within 5 10% of the base salary. Therefore, before negotiating for the signing bonus, get the base salary discussion on the table. There are three main reasons why an employer may give a signing bonus.

1. To show competitiveness against other job offers

2. To bridge a gap of leaving benefits from the organization that a candidate is exiting before receiving a bonus payout

3. To overcome internal salary caps for a position

The third area underscores the importance of talking to men within your industry to find out what's standard. It's rare that these bonuses will appear on the online salary databases. Most signing bonuses come with a clause that you must work for the company for one to two years or risk paying back the bonus amount. Generally, the signing bonus will be paid out within the first month of employment. Before asking for a signing bonus, consider if you're walking away from a bonus at your current employer and what that amount will be.

No, Now What?

The second part of the LATTE method is to anticipate challenges. *No* is a common word in negotiations and should not be feared. Anticipate hearing the word "no" one or more times during the process of negotiating, the word *no* is a signal to get creative; it isn't a final stopping point. If you don't get the result you want, don't give up. Take some time to review what went wrong and what you would do differently next time. However, before going into a deep analysis of the negotiation follow through to the end of the conversation. Often times, the first no is not the end of the conversation. As you negotiate more often, you will understand there will be times as a negotiator you will have to say no and at other times you will be on the receiving end of hearing a no response.

It's ok to say no to a situation where you are the person who's delivering a no. Many women explain in great detail or apologize for saying no but that is not necessary. No, is a complete sentence and can stand on its own. Do not feel obligated to give a detailed explanation. Most women feel guilty for saying no, and therefore, they tend to provide an excessive amount of information to follow-up the no.

Get comfortable saying no and moving forward positively. It is not a matter of politeness or rudeness; it is communicating in a clear and concise matter. As with the other tools you use to negotiate, this is a skill that will be strengthened as you began to engage with it more frequently. Start saying no without explanation in low stakes conversations as a way to build the skill. When you become comfortable saying no without providing an explanation, it will become easier to interject into negotiations. If you decide to give an explanation, provide facts and avoid sharing information that can be misinterpreted. Provide the facts and avoid using language that is descriptive of feelings. Brevity in saying no is a powerful tool to use in communicating throughout negotiations.

In career negotiations, it is common to expect that you will receive a counter-offer if you have declined an initial offer. The details that you share following the no may be used as leverage in the counter offer. Therefore, be mindful in the choice of words you use as well as the tone in which you convey your message. It is worth noting what is said in response to you and what is not said during this time. The time between conversations in the midst of the negotiation can span days to weeks, and this timing is often used as a strategy. Many women get nervous during the time of waiting, and one tool that is helpful during this time is speaking with a mentor or coach who can advise on how to wait. The waiting aspect can be overwhelming and is where many who have followed the steps up until this point cave in and throw in the towel. Don't leave money on the table by giving in because the timing is taking longer than you anticipated. Even when the other party states that they will touch base within a particular time, it can be a couple of weeks before they get back to continuing the negotiations.

When someone responds to your request with a no, get into flow mode. The flow is an acronym that stands for:

- Facts over feelings

- Leverage areas of agreement

- Open the discussion to new ideas

- Walk away if necessary

Facts over feelings

> "If you don't risk anything, you risk even more." - *Erica Jong*

Receiving news that is counter to your desired result can lead to an emotional cloud. In the initial moments of receiving, instead of getting angry, defensive, or feeling sad, pause and take a timeout to evaluate the facts more than you give weight to your feelings. Emotional intelligence is essential to navigating negotiation successfully; however, emotion should not trump judgement, especially when presented with facts. It's okay to feel whatever you feel during the moment of shock; however it is wise to pause before reacting. Your response to disappointing news in a negotiation is a power play, and if you lose control of your emotions, you will give leverage to the other party. During moments of intense emotions, it is a best practice to pause the negotiation by suggesting a break. The break can be a few moments, hours, or days. The length of time of the break should be based on your best judgement of the urgency of the details related to the negotiation. This is a phrase that may be helpful in slowing the negotiation down to gather your thoughts and emotions; tweak it to fit your communication style.

"Okay, let me recap. (Insert a brief summary.) I need some time to process. Let's come back to this conversation in (insert time to resume conversation). Does this work for you?"

By asking a question at the end, you are strategically getting buy-in from the other party as well as showing them that you are coming back to the conversation or negotiation table. Furthermore, your collected response to news you don't want to hear, shows that you're still engaged but less than thrilled by stating disappointment while continuing the discussion. Do not worry if the other party senses some disappointment. It's fine to show disappointment, while not losing your cool.

During your cool off period, reflect on the facts while acknowledging your emotions. You may feel one way that the other party is acting in an unfair manner; therefore, check your emotions by reviewing the facts in the situation. This is a good time to use the five-part LATTE Method.

1. Look at the details from both perspectives

2. Anticipate challenges - did you anticipate this challenge? What solutions did you think in advance of the current reality?

3. Think about your walk way point, are you there?

4. Talk it through - with a trusted mentor or advisor

5. Evaluate all the options before making a decision

Leverage areas of agreement

After you've had ample time to gather your thoughts and go through the LATTE checklist again, go back to the conversation with the goal of reaching a win/win agreement. After all, you and the other party both have something you would like to exchange in value. Don't forget that there is something that both you and the other party wanted from each other that got you in the position to be this far in the conversation.

Revisit areas that both parties have agreed upon by presenting open-ended questions to confirm what you have previously discussed.

Here are a few open-ended question examples you can use to leverage agreement and move past stagnation. No, in negotiations does not mean that the conversation is over, it is a signal to get creative and find ways for you and the other party to walk away with a win/win.

- How can we get back on track? we seem to have hit this speed bump.

- What can we do to move forward? I am still excited about the possibility of making this happen.

- We both want to achieve (insert one are of mutual agreement here). How can we do that at this point?

- The (insert a second area of mutual agree here) is important to you; what timeline do you envision for that?

- What is it that would make you feel comfortable moving forward?

Use this set of questions to help you leverage areas of agreement. Create your own list of questions, and try to expand your questions beyond what would require a simple yes or no response.

Question starters:

- Who

- What

- When

- Where

- How

Open the discussion to new ideas

Throughout strategy and the planning phase, you may have developed ideas on how you would reach an agreement that may have included which factors would be a part of that agreement. However, because things often shift and may not play out exactly the way it was envisioned, be prepared to think outside of the box and find alternative routes to get to the end goal. For example, if you are driving to work and encounter a traffic jam, you don't call and quit your job. Typically, you would use a GPS to find another route. Although it may take longer and be an unfamiliar path to your destination, you adjust accordingly. Similarly in a negotiation when you reach an impasse, you may have to find another route even though it may take longer and may be unfamiliar to get to the desired result.

Open the discussion to new ideas is to practice presenting open-ended questions to gain more information. Information is power; the more you know the better informed decisions you can make. Think outside of the box when formulating these open-ended questions. Using who, what, when, where, and how to formulate questions helps to expand beyond a simple yes or no. The key and using open-ended questions is to expand beyond the current information you have to find out what flexibility the other party has to reach an agreement. It may be helpful to revisit your preparation notes during this phase to refresh on data that you received that may help you expand the view that you currently have of the situation.

Walk away if necessary

The fifth step in the LATTE method is evaluating options. Do not be afraid to walk away if you feel the terms are not acceptable and mutually beneficial. However, walking away should be the final act after you have explored all other options. Walking away is a difficult personal decision and should be made after exploring all the facts. Prior to making the decision to walk away, understand that no is a common term in negotiations and there are ways to be creative to exhaust all possible options before getting to the point of walking away. There is a significant power in knowing you have alternative options even if the only visible option is to walk away. A study shared in the Harvard Business Review showcases how people who imagine they had alternative offers made better decisions in negotiations as compared to those who thought the only option was to accept the offer presented. What that study underscores is the importance of knowing that walking away is an option. For those who feel that they cannot turn down an offer, even if it is not mutually beneficial or does not meet realistic expectations, they are more likely to accept a less than stellar offer. There is always an option even if that option is walking away.

What to do when someone tells you no

Don't become overwhelmed with emotion during the conversation. Negotiations take time and no is a general part of the process. Some negotiations are completed quickly while other negotiations may take months to come to an agreement. Don't get stuck at no. Think past it by referring to the preparation in which you anticipated challenges. The benefit of anticipating the challenges before the negotiation started gives you the advantage of having some solutions that were developed when you were clear headed and did not have as many elevated emotions. Get into the practice of finding solutions through the process of presenting open-ended questions to gather additional information. Information is power; the more you know about the circumstances you will be able to make well-informed decisions.

There are few questions that are useful to keep the conversation moving beyond the "NO."

1. Ask under what circumstances would they be able to say "yes"?

2. Ask if any exceptions have ever been made?

3. Ask is this the best we can do?

4. What can we do to get back on the same page?

What questions can you list that will help you move beyond "No"?

Emulating Excellence

> "Emulate Excellence and Nix All Excuses" ~ *Jacqueline V. Twillie*

Top earners crush it consistently; they go in every day and give it their all, regardless of how they feel. To earn what you are worth, you must be known as the person who gets the job done, not the person who can start but doesn't finish, not the person who complains but eventually does the work, and not the person, who if no one else is around, you can get them to work on the project. Emulating Excellence does not mean you have to be perfect, but it does suggest that you go hard every day! Examine the excuses you tell yourself that prevent you from giving 110% in all you do. Often times, people say there is not enough time to get things done, yet upon deep reflection or analysis or smartphone usage there is a common thread of five minutes here or there that is spent without knowing. A popular cliché says time is money, but time is more valuable than money because once time is used there is no way to recover it. As you look for ways to eliminate excuses so that you don't leave money on the table, it will require you to examine your relationship with excellence on a consistent basis. Aristotle is credited with saying, "We are what we repeatedly do. Excellence, then, is not an act, but a habit." Top earners are known as problem solvers, those who get things done even in the midst of adversity. Negotiation is just as much about your reputation to be excellent at what you do, as it is about saying the "right" things during the negotiation. Look for ways to increase your effectiveness at work and in the community. By increasing your reputation for excellence, you increase the leverage you have to ask for more and negotiate for more.

Change is difficult for most people, and those who learn to embrace change, whether in technology or business, increase their leadership profile. Do you have the same attitude about your work and worth? Are you emulating excellence at a level that you can confidently ask for compensation related to the value you deliver and request the appropriate rate so that you're not leaving any money on the table?

How serious are you about earning what you are worth? Create a list of 5 action items you can take to emulate excellence and eliminate excuses.

Performance Review

> "Know who you are and what you are skilled at. Be clear on your career aspirations. Know the value you add and articulate that clearly."
> *-Jacqueline V. Twillie*

In advance of presenting a request to a supervisor or manager for more responsibility and money, prepare thoroughly for your review. A primary factor is knowing the value you add to the team and company. In addition to knowing the value you add, be able to articulate that value in the lingo that is relevant to the company goals and key performance indicators. Go beyond the standard template that your company may have and analyze the work you have done. It is your primary responsibility to articulate the value you add. Most supervisors and managers have many responsibilities and as a result, even the managers with the best intentions for your career growth may forget the contributions that you have made within the fiscal year. What are your major wins since your last review or since you started in the position? Do you go above and beyond on a noticeably consistent basis? If you do not share what you're doing, it could go unnoticed and unrewarded. If you do not share your career aspirations, it is difficult for those around you to advocate and support you in making career moves.

A helpful tool to keep track of the work that you complete in a fiscal year is having a physical brag folder or an electronic file on your personal device that includes positive feedback as well as significant contributions that can be added to a resume or LinkedIn profile. It may be helpful to update this record quarterly; as time goes on, it becomes difficult to capture the full scope of the project you may be contributing to. Along with the contributions to the team and company, record professional development activities such as completed courses or professional association membership involvement as well as conferences in the summary of activities to include during a performance discussion. Equally as important as success or acknowledgement are lessons learned from possible mistakes. It's better to be proactive and think through key takeaways from constructive feedback or mistakes that were made with action steps already in play to improve moving forward.

In preparation for a performance discussion, always follow the company protocol incorporating these additional steps as an awareness tool for you and a career map to help articulate the value you add as well as the career aspirations you have. If the company doesn't have a formal review process, use a template to help you guide the conversation. If you are asking for additional monetary compensation, keep the fiscal calendar in mind as budgets may be determined on a timeline outside of the time of your request.

A part of the preparation for the performance review is a self-assessment of how you receive feedback but positive as well as constructive. Many women have a tendency to downplay positive feedback, therefore, devaluing their contributions to the team or company. Phrases such as:

- Oh, you don't have to thank me for that

- That's no big deal

- I can do that in my sleep

- Don't mention it

- Oh, that was easy

- Don't worry about it

- Anyone would have done it

The above phrases are all too common and devaluing statements that can impact the perception of your contributions and performance at review time. If you have used these phrases in the past, become more mindful of it and move to more empowering statements that claim value. Phrases such as:

- Thank you

- I appreciate you recognizing that

- I pride myself on doing that well

- I appreciate the positive feedback

- I dedicate a lot of time to ensure this is completed in an excellent manner

- It's nice to be recognized; this is something I'm

very proud of

- I'm proud to do this work

- Great, thanks for the feedback

Add three value claiming statements to this list that you can begin to use when you receive positive affirmations on your work.

1.

2.

3.

Small changes related to how you communicate about the work you deliver can significantly impact how you are perceived within the organization. Be mindful at all times of, both verbal and written communications of value-adding or devaluing statements that you used to describe your work ethic. This is another tool that can be strengthened over time, and the more you engage in it the stronger it will become. Self-awareness is a driving factor in recognizing this language because many of the deep value in phrases come without much intention. Consciously begin to give awareness to your thoughts, especially when it relates to your communication about your professionalism.

Starting the conversation to ask for more responsibility and compensation can cause nervousness. The following is an example of phrases that can be used in the conversation with your supervisor. It's beneficial to create your own outline and use language that is natural to your personality style. Practice what you want to say aloud prior to having the conversation with your supervisor. If possible, record yourself and watch the video or listen to the audio so that you can see and hear how you sound.

There may be areas that you want to polish prior to going into the conversation.

Asking for a title change and salary increase,

Say: Thank you for recognizing my contributions to the team. When I get emails from you, my peers, and the clients, it reminds me of why I love this department. I'd like to dive deep into some of the feedback you've shared with me over the past year and discuss ways to increase my contribution in the next fiscal year.

As I prepared for this meeting, I realized I've worked on 20 projects in the past year, meeting and exceeding goals on 84% of those projects. One of the things you mentioned to me was that I clogged your inbox by cc'ing you on numerous emails. I have a solution to that problem. I've cc'd you on so many emails because I have to prove that I have the permission/authority to request specific information and having your name on the email chain has allowed me access to important data to complete my job function. If my title were to change, it would allow my internal and external partners to know that I have authority to request such information which will free up your inbox. Along with that, I'd welcome the bump in pay to match the title and work responsibility. You also mentioned that during the weather emergency, my productivity levels soared while I worked from home. I also noticed the spike in my productivity absent of the distractions. What will it take for us to make this a part of my bi-weekly work schedule?

Create your own outline for the conversation that you envision.

Do not be discouraged if your initial request is not approved right away. There are several factors that go into a company approving a request for more responsibility and compensation; therefore, realistically set your expectations and discuss the details of a plan and outline with your supervisor if it isn't possible to make a transition in the next three to six months. By clarifying the timeline beyond the six-month window as well as gaining an understanding of what steps need to be taken on your end to make the transition to more responsibility in job duties along increased compensation

As you progress in your career, continue to hone those skills by keeping current with certifications and market trends. Invest in yourself by attending conferences and subscribing to industry publications. These things, combined with your performance and network, will be leveraged to continue to earn top dollar in your salary. Be clear on your career aspirations, even if they change. It is up to you to be able to articulate that to the people who are advocating and supporting your career and leadership development.

You are in the driver's seat of your career. The actions you take today are laying the foundation of where you will be in the future. Are you going big in your leadership journey? Are you taking risks? Are you being fearless? It can be so hard to take risks and to be fearless because we usually don't want to make mistakes, and we don't want to look bad. For women leaders in male-dominated industries, you have so much to prove already, and on top of that, you just don't want to let yourself down. A lot of you have very high standards for yourself. But when was the last time you've taken a risk at work and done something new for the very first time? As you build your leadership profile, leverage these seven points of insight as a catalyst to inspire you to step into your power and play big as a leader.

1. Get comfortable with the concept of failure

2. Get up after failure and keep moving

3. Take inspired action and always have support

4. Try again and again and again

5. Surround yourself with people who will push you to be the highest and grandest version of yourself

6. Go big or go home; if you're going to put yourself out there do your best

7. Enjoy the journey

Part of enjoying the process as a leader is knowing that sometimes you learn more in a challenging situation. You are forced to think more creatively and think outside of the box. Breaking your own rules and learning how to expand your thought patterns using negotiation skills to help you advocate for yourself, your team, and company so that you are not leaving money on the table. Your performance review(s) should be more than a tool used for a company to evaluate how you are doing; it should be a check-in with yourself to gauge where you are as compared to where you want to be. Take ownership of this process.

Executive Presence & Negotiation

> "People respond well to those that are sure of what they want."
> *— Anna Wintour*

Knowing your value is a powerful concept and phrase, one that gets thrown around very loosely. A lot of people use the phrase, know your value, but when it comes to your workplace and knowing your value in the workplace, it's about understanding how you solve problems and how you contribute in a meaningful way to achieve big goals. So each company, when they hire an employee, whether it is the CEO or someone on the entry-level, they're hiring that person to fill a gap. There is a problem that company is trying to solve, and they need a person in that position to actually go through and do the work. That's where the employee comes in. Again, doesn't matter what level you're on. At each level, there are expectations, doing the bare minimum at work isn't enough to request an increase in pay. That's what the paycheck is for. You're paid to do the work, but when you go above and beyond, and when you start to deliver exceptional value to the organization, that's where you get to go in and ask for a promotion or a raise or more responsibility or to be placed on special assignments and tied to a bigger bonus.

In male-dominated industries, how women are perceived, most of the time, is tied to their communication skills and their ability to relate with others as leaders. Therefore, it is important that women learn to communicate and claim their rightful place at the negotiation table. Without good and effective communication skills, women will fail to command a room and will not make people stop and listen to what they have to say. Executive presence and negotiation is a huge cornerstone for women leaders, especially within male dominated industries. The skills of commanding attention, delivering a message, and solving problems translate to any industry. For women who want to have a lasting impact in their leadership, executive presence could be the key they need to help attain their goals; recognizing the importance of how executive presence plays into leadership strategy and what that has to do with negotiation. Leveraging executive presence and negotiation sets a strong foundation of becoming a more effective leader while allowing you as a leader to produce results for a company. As you step more into your power as leader in a traditionally male-dominated industry, overcoming stereotypes becomes a daily practice but should be secondary to achieving the goals and objectives needed to move the organization forward.

Five steps to enhance executive presence:

1. Self-awareness drives behavior in claiming

agency to lead

2. Self-efficacy is the antidote to imposter syndrome

3. Get comfortable with power

4. Ask probing questions regularly

5. Integrity is a cornerstone for leadership success

Step one, self-awareness drives behavior in claiming agency as you lead. Executive presence captures several skills, the most important being awareness of self. Knowing how you show up to others and the perception of who you are as a leader helps you to navigate situations in a savvy manner. There is an old saying that holds true, "perception is reality." The way in which other people perceive your leadership drives many decisions when you are not in the room, even with a leadership title. Increasing the skill of self-awareness can be done by taking time to reflect on attitudes habits and actions.

AHA Method

A: Actions - Actions you engage in on a daily basis that influence those around you. What unintentional messages are you sending through your actions? Some people say actions speak louder than words; therefore, evaluating if your actions and words are aligned can be beneficial in increasing self-awareness.

H: Habits - The previous section of the book we talked about emulating excellence and how excellence is a habit. Notice what has become routine for you, whether it's how you start your day or how you communicate within meetings, these habits are often indicative of how you learn and provide context to others on how they should engage with you. Becoming aware and being intentional about habits increases executive presence.

A: Attitude - Stress in leadership roles is common, however, an unintended consequence of stress is the impact on one's attitude. Awareness of your attitude and both stressful and non-stressful situations can help you control how you show up in meetings which is directly correlated with executive presence.

Step two, self- efficacy is the antidote to the imposter syndrome. Self-efficacy is your ability to control your emotions. As with other leadership skills, this is one that is counter to having a strong executive presence. The online dictionary explains self-efficacy as an individual's belief in their innate ability to achieve goals. Albert Bandura is credited with coining this phrase, and he defines it as a personal judgment of "how well one can execute courses of action required to deal with prospective situations." Often the imposter syndrome is a driving factor for women leaders to second-guess decisions. It's common to hear this topic come up at women's conferences, and the most common phrase is one similar to this, "I wonder am I good enough" or "are people going to think I'm a fraud?" By elevating the executive presence skill, you will find that these thoughts have to be dismissed and thrown out of the window if you're going to have executive presence. Recognize that no one achieved anything great by doubling down on the self-limiting thoughts associated with the imposter syndrome. Your ability to tap into awareness of everything around you and to understand which skills are needed in the moment is your efficacy in action. To exert leadership in a moment when you know you have the knowledge and skills to lead effectively is a power claiming move. For others to follow you confidently, you've first have to prove you are confident in your actions. Work towards achieving a level of mastery where you stand in agency and defeat the imposter syndrome.

Step three, get comfortable with power. You have agency just by being in the room. In the previous step, self-efficacy is the antidote to imposter syndrome. Taking that further is getting comfortable with power. Power has received a negative connotation, in part due to the glamorization of those who have power and have done bad things, whether it's politics, business, even in movies and television shows. There are examples of positive use of power, and for many women, it is worth studying those who are effective in using power to be a positive catalyst. Examining your industry leaders historical figures can help the framework of stepping into the agency you have to be an effective leader as well as showing up as your most confident self.

Step four, ask probing questions regularly. Listening is just as important as speaking to executive presence. The ability to formulate probing questions is a hallmark of women who own their executive presence. Develop the skills for asking probing questions by engaging in active listening, coupled with the ability to conceive open-ended questions. By using this two-pronged approach, frequently it showcases thought leadership as well as underscores your problem-solving ability.

Step five, integrity is the cornerstone to executive presence, leading, and negotiation success. What you say and do when no one is watching becomes even more important in leadership and negotiations in the digital age. While Integrity has always been important, the scrutiny from online platforms can amplify even the slightest missteps. Reviewing your values on a consistent basis and speaking to the team that you directly lead, enhances executive presence.

Negotiation FAQS

> You gain strength, courage, and confidence by every experience in which you really stop to look fear in the face. You are able to say to yourself, 'I lived through this horror. I can take the next thing that comes along." -Eleanor Roosevelt

This list of questions and answers are the most common questions presented to the author of this book.

Q: How do I answer the question how much do you make now?

A: When answering the question related to your current salary, keep in mind that in some US states it is illegal to require a job applicant to disclose previous salary data. However, in the states where it is still legal for an employer to request such information provide the salary expectations for the role you are interviewing for. It is key to focus on your salary expectation for the job that you want, not your current or previous role. The reason is that women are paid less than men in almost every industry, and to use a benchmark that is already below the market rate in terms of a new position, continues to perpetuate the cycle of being underpaid. Therefore, conduct market research to determine what the proper rate is and state your salary expectations based on the job description and the expected work.

Q: What should I do if I'm afraid of negotiating?

A: If you're nervous, that's ok. Feel the fear and prepare to ask confidently. If you don't ask, you won't get. Practice what you want to say aloud, even recording and playing back what you'd like to say on your smartphone so that you can tweak how you sound.

Q: How can a woman prepare for an ask, and then how can she crush it?

A: Prepare for an ask by coming to the table with the facts surrounding your performance that fall in line with company goals.

Items of things to consider:

- Metrics that are important to your manager (the things they mention in emails and meetings)

- Industry trends that directly influence your work

- Market data on base salary, bonuses, retirement matches, and other company perks such as

- Student loan repayment plans.

- Write an outline of what you'd like to ask for and practice aloud

- Anticipate curve balls and possible no's and create a game plan response

- If you get a "no", don't give up asking if any exceptions have ever been made

Q: When is it time to ask for a raise? (Three indicators)

A: Every business will have their own metrics for giving raises. A few indicators that may signal it's time for a raise is increased responsibility after successfully completing challenging projects over an extended period of time, such as 3-5 business quarters. Another indicator may be a change in supervisor responsibility; an example is managing a team that drives revenue for the organization when you were previously just responsible for yourself. A third possible indicator that it is time to request a raise is that you are increasing the value you deliver to the organization; this will depend on your role and the industry you are in, so pay attention to major wins that you contribute to on your team and within the company as a whole. It is important to recognize that you can only ask for a raise if you're performing at a high level and adding value to the organization. Time in position is an indicator of seeking a raise.

Q: How can women find out how much they should be paid for a certain job or career?

A: Speak to your network or white males according to the latest wage gap data. They get paid the most in the U.S. across many industries. You can start the research prior to a conversation by looking up salary data online at @PayScale, @Glassdoor, and professional association data. Include all relevant details, and be sure to include the geographic location. The location impacts the market rate.

Q: What mistakes do young professionals make when

taking a job offer or negotiating?

A: A few mistakes that young professionals make when accepting a job offer is asking for an amount that is out of sync with the current market rate or accepting the first offer without exploring if it is the best possible offer. Negotiating young professionals should spend time researching the issues at hand, common areas of interest, possible conflict areas, and ways to creatively bridge the gap to end up with a win/win. For example, when negotiating for a title change, think of what's in it for you and the employer, and when you have the discussion, lead with what's in it for the company to increase the chances of getting what you want.

Q: What if you were not prepared with the market rate?

A: If you don't know the market rate, when asked what your salary expectations are, respond by asking what the salary range is for this role. Then pause, there is a tendency to want to explain why you are asking the salary range, but you don't need to justify why you are asking. You should prepare as much as possible so that you are armed with the facts, such as what the market rate is for the position. The more you know about the company and role it increases your chances of earning the top rate.

Q: Is there a "nice" way to negotiate?

A: Negotiation is not about niceness. However, when you negotiate, you are negotiating with a person, so keep in mind professional rules of engagement. You want to keep a professional decorum throughout the conversation. It is better to be respected and firm than nice and a pushover. Industries in communities are small; you will establish a reputation in business for your negotiation style over a period of time. Be mindful of this because this can be used as others prepare to negotiate with you.

Q: What are some of the things that women need to ask for when negotiating or asking for a raise?

A: In addition to negotiating for money, there are many professional items to be considered. This can expand to any resources or support that aids you to be successful in the role. Think of software equipment, professional development, and association memberships and conferences as just a few of those resources.

- Vacation time

- Start date

- Exit terms

- Remote work dates

- Sabbatical terms

- Parental leave

- Student loan repayment

- Tuition assistance

- Performance review evaluation timeframe

This is not an exhaustive list just a few ideas to help you get the wheels turning.

Q: Which one can guarantee more pay, a degree in higher education or job experience?

A: It is a combination and depends on the job. Focus on your track record of success as it relates to the job you are negotiating salary. If you're switching industries, past success is an indicator of future success. Speak to the value you'll add through transferable skills. The key is to meet the needs of the company. As more companies move away from requiring degrees, it is more important to understand what skills or certifications are required to land the job.

Q: How should women deal with the disappointment of being told 'no' when they ask for a promotion or raise?

A: Negotiation is a skill that gets better when put into practice. Learn from each negotiation and make adjustments the next time. "There are no secrets to success. It is the result of preparation, hard work, and learning from failure." ~ Colin Powell

Q: Should college graduates negotiate pay for their first job?

A: YES! "By not negotiating a first salary, an individual stands to lose more than $500,000 by age 60."

"...and men are more than four times as likely as women to negotiate a first salary." ~ Sara Lascaver

Q: Is it necessary to bring up one's last job salary amount when negotiating an offer?

A: If you were paid at market rate and are doing a similar type of work, it may be relevant to share. However, if you were not paid at market rate, focus your salary negotiation on what the market rate is for your experience, education, and skill level. As data shows, women are paid less. In most cases, past salary isn't a true marker for what you should be paid moving forward.

Q: What are three tips for becoming a successful negotiator?

A: The top tips for becoming a successful negotiator are learning to listen, preparing thoroughly, and having a plan for when things go off track. Using the five-part LATTE method as your framework for strategy will elevate the skills you already possess. As you become more confident in your negotiation skills, revisit this book to discover additional ways to elevate the skillset.

Q: Are there any materials or sources that I should use (or cite) as support when negotiating compensation?

A: When speaking about compensation, the market rate can be cited as well as any verifiable data you gained during the research phase step one in the LATTE method, looking at the details. It is wise to avoid sharing any personal financial obligations as the main cause for requesting an increase. When sharing information of another offer from another party, use caution in the level of detail and do not embellish the number.

Q: What challenges can I anticipate facing when trying to negotiate compensation?

A: Challenges will vary based on company, department, or team. Using self-awareness and gathering data from available resources, whether online or through your network, will help you to create a realistic list of challenges you may face. Once you identify any possible challenges, consider how you will overcome them.

Q: What are the necessary steps to take after a successful negotiation, e.g. draft a follow-up note to confirm what was discussed, etc.?

A: After a negotiation, whether successful or unsuccessful, a best practice is to evaluate the performance and consider what you would do moving forward.

What will you start doing in future negotiations?

What will you stop doing in negotiations?

What did you learn from the negotiation?

Q: How many rounds of negotiations are appropriate

to reach your desired compensation?

A: There isn't a set rule on how many rounds of negotiation it will take to reach a desired compensation. Some negotiations are done very quickly, while others may take days or weeks. It's important to ask clarifying questions throughout the process. Gauge the timeline of the party you're negotiating with. In the process of waiting as you go back and forth in negotiation, keep all of your options on the table, and don't close alternative doors until an agreement has been reached.

Q: How can you negotiate if you are re-entering the workforce after taking some time off?

A: In chapter one of the book, we discussed the importance of knowing your value and confidently articulating the value you bring to the table. When negotiating re-entry to the workforce, it is important to showcase any skills that were enhanced or developed during the time away. There are several work reentry programs that provide training on how to enhance skills if perhaps you did not intentionally develop skills during the time from work. For women who take time off to care for children or elderly family members, talk about the transferable skills of managing a home and the effective use of attention to detail as well as time management. Oftentimes, old skills are very necessary in the workforce, and depending on the position that you're applying to, couple that with your previous experience to build a stronger case for you to receive the appropriate market rate.

Q: What do you need to prepare to negotiate salary, and when is the right time?

A: Follow the five-part LATTE method to create a negotiation strategy. Don't skip any of the steps as each has a role in developing a strong strategy to present the facts and confidently make a decision. 80% of the negotiation is in the preparation.

Q: Why are most women scared to ask for more money?

A: Fear is one of the reasons why women don't negotiate. Contributing factors to fear are often: not knowing how to ask, fear of rejection, not knowing if it's acceptable to ask, or fear that the offer will be rescinded if you counter. Refer back to the section in the book that is a tool for overcoming fears using affirmation is one catalyst to overcome. The purpose of this book in its entirety is to lay the foundation and best practices for women work within male-dominated industries so that they don't leave money on the table. If you don't ask, the answer will always be no. It is rare that the first offer is the best offer; therefore, it's worth negotiating and at minimum asking, "Is this the best we can do?"

LATTE
Negotiation
Checklist

Your objective: _____
_____
_____
_____
_____
_____
_____
_____

- Look at the details

- Anticipate the challenges

- Think about the walk away point

- Talk it through

- Evaluate the options

About the author

Jacqueline V. Twillie holds an M.B.A. in Leadership, she is the Founder and President of ZeroGap.co, a global training, and development firm that specializes in women's leadership within male-dominated industries.ZeroGap has been identified as one of the fastest growing companies in 2019 by Inc. Jacqueline is an <u>Amazon Best Selling Author</u>She has been featured in <u>Forbes</u>, <u>FastCo</u>, <u>Essence Now</u> , <u>Black Enterprise</u> , <u>Parade</u> , Today. com, <u>NBC BLK</u> and more... on the topic of Women's Leadership and Negotiation Strategy.

Jacqueline is a graduate of <u>Southeastern Louisiana University</u> and earned her MBA from Tiffin University. Her life's mission is to eliminate the gender wage gap by providing practical strategy for women to advance and thrive in leadership roles. In her downtime, she loves to practice yoga and cook. When Jacqueline isn't working on leadership development for women she enjoys seeing the world from up in the air check out her <u>skydive video on YouTube</u>.